Introducing
MAPS

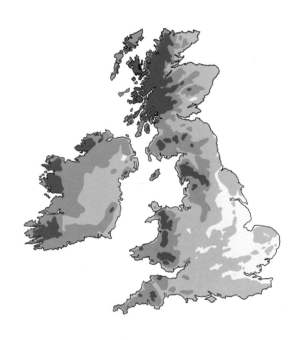

Jack and Meg Gillett

Published in paperback in 2014 by Wayland
Copyright © Wayland 2014

Wayland
338 Euston Road
London NW1 3BH

Wayland Australia
Hachette Children's Books
Level 17/207 Kent Street
Sydney, NSW 2000

Managing Editor: Rasha Elsaeed
Editor: Katie Dicker
Picture researcher: Shelley Noronha
Designer: Alix Wood. Illustrator: Catherine Ward
Author dedication: 'For Jade'

Picture Credits
Front cover, top left: © Skyscan / A Hunter. Page 4,
Figure A: Jacques Descloitres, MODIS Land Rapid
Response Team, NASA / GSFC. Page 5,
Figure B: © Skyscan. Page 5, Figure C: Martyn Chillmaid. Page 6, Figure A: © Skyscan / A Hunter. Page 6, Figure B: Skyscan /
Imagery
© Getmapping plc. Page 8, Figure A: ©TopFoto. Page 23, Figure C: Based on OS Sheet 154 Landranger Map 1:50 000
Cambridge and Newmarket. Page 27, Figure B: Jack & Meg Gillett.

Page 21 and 30 may be reproduced for class use solely within the purchaser's school or college.
Note to parents and teachers: Every effort has been made by the publishers to ensure that websites referred to in the book are
suitable for children. However, because of the nature of the Internet, it is impossible to guarantee that the contents of these sites
will not be altered. We strongly advise that Internet access is supervised by a responsible adult.

British Library Cataloguing in Publication Data
 Gillett, Jack
   Introducing maps. – (Maps and mapping skills)
   1. Map reading – Juvenile literature 2. Map drawing –
   Juvenile literature
   I. Title II. Gillett, Meg
   912'.014

ISBN 978 0 7502 8473 8

Printed in China

10 9 8 7 6 5 4 3 2

Wayland is a division of Hachette Children's Books, an Hachette UK Company
www.hachette.co.uk

Contents

What is a map? .4

Aerial photographs 6

What's on a map? 8

Distance and scale 10

Zooming in 12

How to make a scale plan 14

Map signs and symbols 16

Getting your bearings 18

Four-figure grid references 20

Six-figure grid references 22

Different kinds of maps 24

How to make your own map 26

Use your skills: Island adventure 28

Use your skills: Wordsearch 30

Glossary 31

Index and answers 32

What is a map?

Maps are drawings that show where places are and how they look. Maps are very useful in our lives. We use maps at school, at work and in our leisure time. Like all drawings, maps are flat images of the real, three-dimensional world.

We use maps to find our way around. Maps can also be used to compare different **landscapes**. Maps aren't ordinary drawings – they are illustrated in a special way. Most importantly, maps are drawings of places viewed from above – as seen from a **bird's eye view**. To see places in this way, we have to take a trip in a hot air balloon, a plane or even a spaceship! As we go higher, we see more and more of the Earth's surface (Figure A).

Large and small maps

Some maps show small, local areas, like the view we get from a small plane or a hot air balloon (Figure B). These maps can show lots of detailed information, such as the size of buildings, the bends in a road and the height of the land. Other maps show much larger areas, such as those seen from a plane cruising at 10,000 metres. Maps of larger areas can even show the outline of countries. But these maps show fewer small **features**.

Maps also show landscapes in special ways. Instead of being real-life drawings, maps use colours, abbreviations and **symbols** to show the features that make up a landscape (Figure D). This means that even the smallest maps can show lots of useful information. Maps are a vital tool to help us discover more about the world around us.

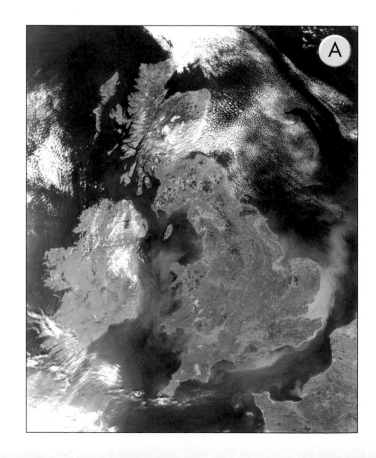

This satellite photograph shows the British Isles from a height of about 36,000 km. The higher we fly, the less detail we see. ▶

▲ This photograph is taken from a plane at about 200 metres. Just above the ground, places can be seen very clearly.

Do it yourself

1 Draw separate bird's eye views of the plate, the cup and saucer, and the teapot shown in Figure C.

2 Now draw a bird's eye view of the whole tea set shown in Figure C.

Maps are a way of drawing different views from above. This map shows features such as roads, buildings, woods and rivers. ▶

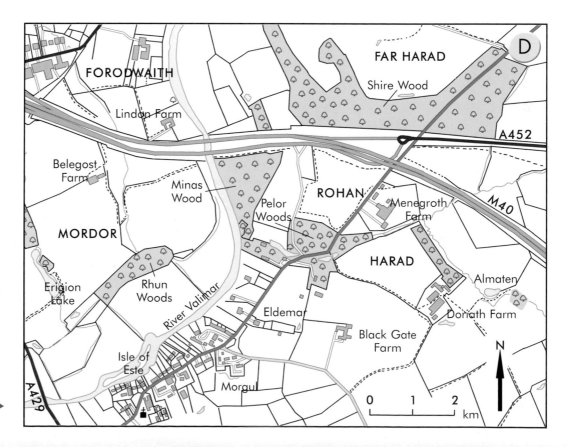

5

Aerial photographs

When photographs are taken from a bird's eye view we call them **aerial photographs**. These photographs are taken above the ground, from a plane or a hot air balloon. There are two main types – oblique photographs and vertical photographs.

Figure A is an oblique photograph of central Durham, taken by a camera looking downwards but at an angle (see Figure C). The vertical photograph of Durham in Figure B, taken looking straight down, is very different. Oblique photographs show information very clearly, but in a vertical photograph it's difficult to recognise anything other than street patterns and the shapes of big features such as lakes and woods.

Using vertical photographs

Roads, buildings and other landscape features look much simpler when viewed directly from above. Although it is difficult to recognise the familiar buildings of a city or a town from this angle, the location of main features can be clearly seen. Modern map-makers use vertical photographs to help them produce clear maps that show the size and location of the features of an area.

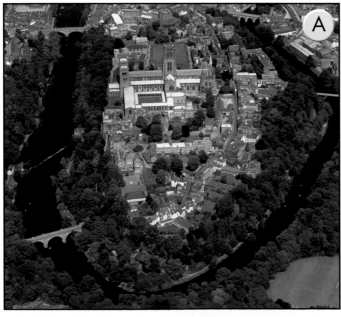

▲ *This is an oblique photograph of central Durham. You can see the cathedral clearly.*

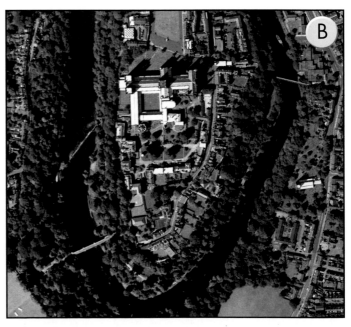

▲ *This is a vertical photograph of central Durham. The cathedral is now seen as an outline.*

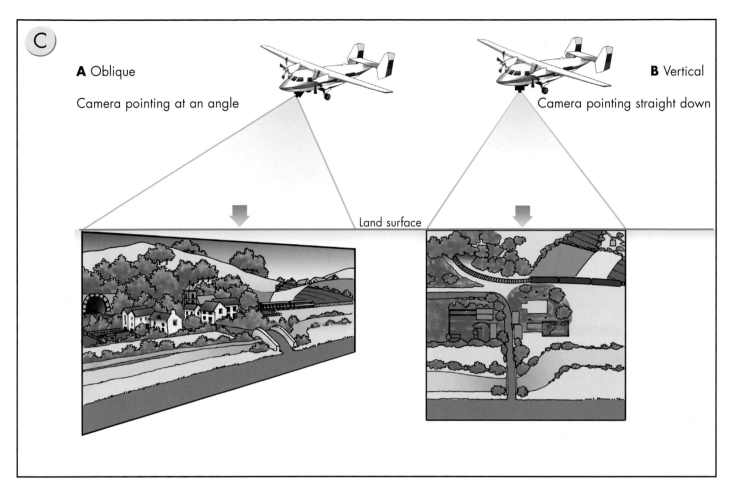

A Oblique

Camera pointing at an angle

B Vertical

Camera pointing straight down

Land surface

▲ *Planes can be used to take oblique and vertical aerial photographs.*

Turning things into a map

Figure C is an illustrated example of the type of oblique and vertical photographs taken by a plane. The area of land surface shown in each photograph is different because of the camera's angle. Notice how the illustrated vertical photograph is beginning to look like a map – you can see the bend in the river, the outline of the houses and an area of green trees. A map of this area would provide even more information – you might be able to see the name of the village, the road and the river, and also the height of the land.

Do it yourself

Take a photograph (or a set of photographs) of your classroom or bedroom.

1 Use the photographs to help you draw a bird's eye view of the room. Use realistic colours to shade it in.

2 What would you need to add to your drawing to turn it into a map?

3 What parts of your illustration have you found most difficult to draw from a bird's eye view?

What's on a map?

Long ago, maps were drawn very differently to the modern maps of today. Before hot air balloons were invented, people had no way of looking at the landscape from above, so they were unable to create a bird's eye view.

Instead of drawing vertical views, early map-makers drew what they could see at ground level. Buildings were shown as seen from the front – complete with doors, windows and roofs (see Figure A). But once it was possible to view the land from above, **cartographers** (map-makers) began to illustrate their maps in a very different way.

Maps only include permanent landscape features such as buildings, roads, rivers and forests. People and traffic are not included on the map in Figure C, for example. These details would be constantly changing! Maps also show buildings as simple, box-like shapes, leaving out details about what they really look like.

Modern maps

Today, map-makers get most of the information they need from aerial photographs that show a bird's eye view of the landscape. However, map-makers still need to visit an area because photographs do not show any detail about the height and shape of the land.

Maps can never show everything in a landscape, so cartographers have to decide what to include and what to leave out.

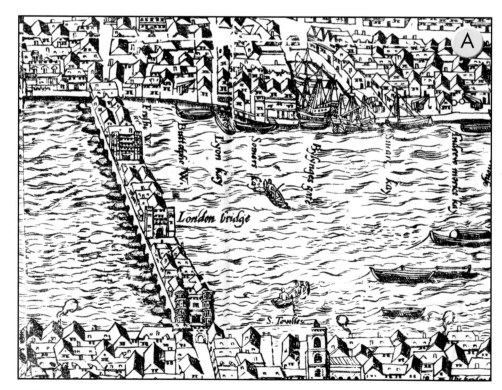

▲ This 16th-century map of London shows the buildings from a ground-level view.

The drawing in Figure B shows central Durham as seen from a bird's eye view. Just like the vertical photograph on page 6, the location of many features can be seen, such as the river and the cathedral.

In contrast, the drawing in Figure C is a map of central Durham. This drawing includes extra information, such as the names of roads and buildings, that might be useful to us.

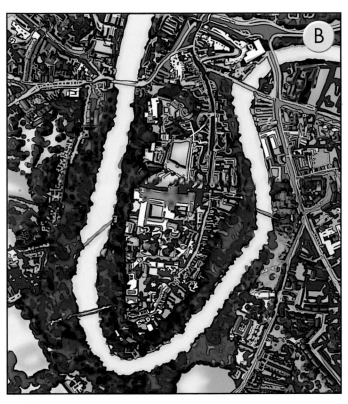

▲ An aerial-view drawing of central Durham, showing the river and cathedral clearly.

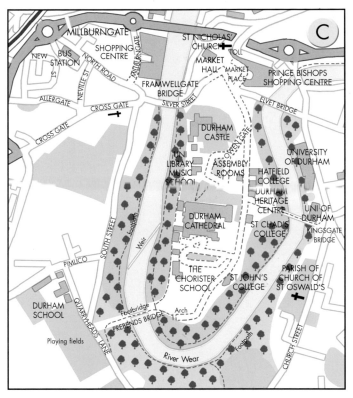

▲ A map of central Durham. This drawing is full of additional information.

Do it yourself

Draw a very old-style map of a small area near to your home or school.

1. Take a sheet of white paper and make it look old – blot it with a cold tea bag to turn it brown and tear the edges slightly.

2. When the paper is dry, start with a street **plan** of a few local roads. Study the buildings carefully and then draw them on your map showing their front-on view. Add some roads or paths.

3. Add colours and labels to make your map look authentic. You could also write some labels using an ink pen and an 'old-fashioned' style script.

Distance and scale

Maps help us to work out how far places are from each other. But to do this, we need to be able to measure map distances accurately. When maps are drawn, the area is reduced to fit onto a piece of paper. The **scale** tells us what this distance is in real-life.

Scale can be shown on a map in three ways. We usually use 'line scales' to measure straight or curved distances. However, we can also use a ruler to measure distances on a map. The 'statement of scale' shows us how far these distances are in real life. Finally, 'ratio scales' tell us how many times the measurement on a map would need to be multiplied, to equal the real-life distance. Some maps use a combination of these scales.

How to use a line scale to measure distances on a map

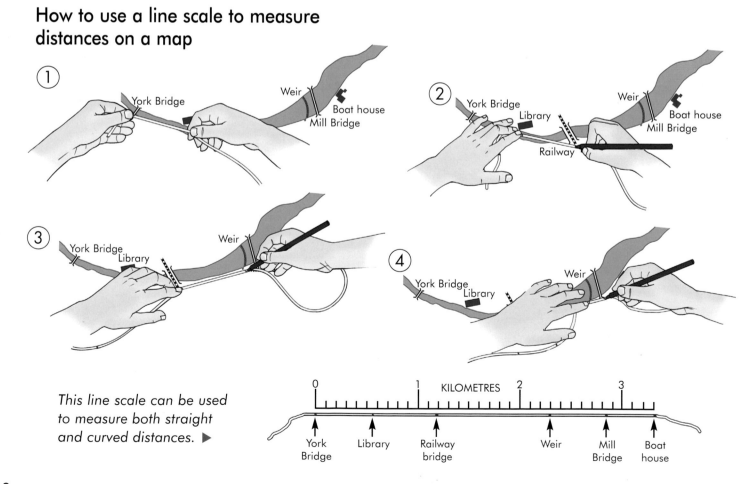

This line scale can be used to measure both straight and curved distances. ▶

Type of scale	Example of scale	Explanation
Line scale	KILOMETRES 0 1 2 3	This line drawing shows what the real-life distance is. You can measure a distance on the map and use the line scale to convert it into kilometres.
Statement of scale	1 cm represents 1 km	This sentence tells you that every centimetre on the map stands for one kilometre in real-life.
Ratio scale	1:50,000	This scale tells you how many times smaller a map is than an area in real-life. A scale of 1:50,000 means that 1 cm would be 50,000 cm (or 500 m) – the length of five football pitches, for example.

Do it yourself

1 Find these distances on the map of the Deepdale Wood area.

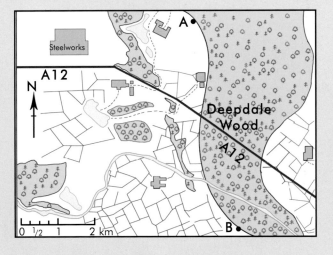

a The length of the steelworks building along its longest side.

b The distance along the A12 main road from where it enters Deepdale Wood to where it leaves it.

c The distance along the A12 main road across the whole of the map.

d The length of the curved side of the wood between points A and B.

e How far is the width of the map in real life?

f How far is the height of the map (from the bottom left corner to the top left corner) in real life?

g What is the total area of the map in real life (in km²)?

Zooming in

Maps can be drawn to show any size of area – map-makers simply shrink things down by the same amount so the important details can fit onto a piece of paper. We call this **scaling-down**.

Maps use colour shadings and special symbols to make particular features easier to see. Different types of roads are shown in colour, built-up areas are shaded and landscape features are added. Map-makers always try to use realistic colours if they can, such as green for woodland, and blue for water features, such as rivers, lakes and sea.

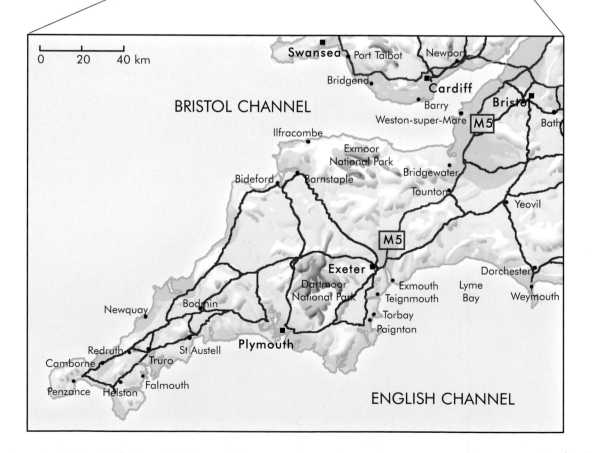

▲ *This map shows the British Isles. You can see the borders of each country and the capital cities.*

This is a map of south-west England. You can see the roads and main towns, as well as landscape features, such as hills and National Parks. ▶

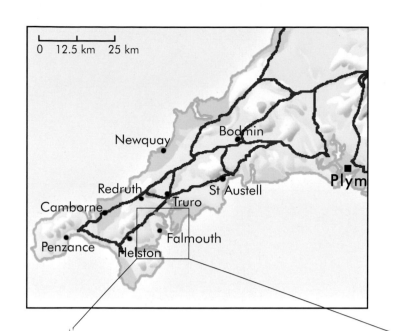

1 Find a map of the street where you live using the website **http://maps.google.co.uk**

2 Practise zooming in and out of the image to see the map at different scales. You could add a print-out of some of these maps to your map collection!

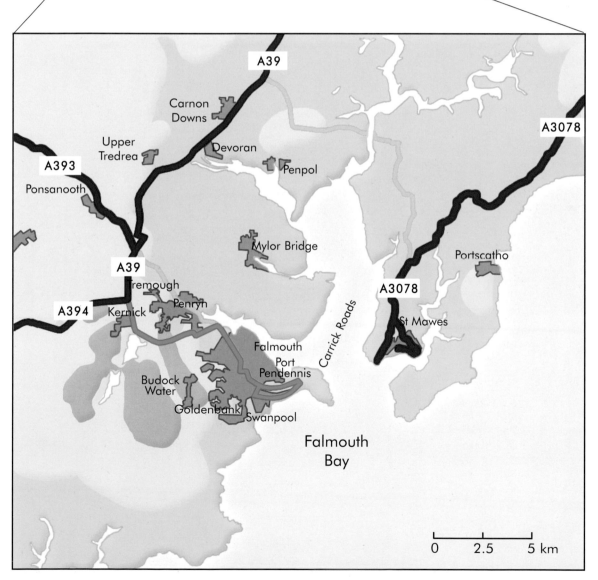

◄ *This map shows the area around the town of Falmouth. You can see towns and villages, the numbers of some roads and the shape of the bay.*

How to make a scale plan

Here's an opportunity to practise your measuring and drawing skills, by making a scale plan of your classroom, your favourite room at home or even the whole of one floor of your house.

1 Copy this table, with one row for each wall of your room.

Wall	Measured length of wall (in m)	Scaled-down length of wall (in cm)
1st		
2nd		

2 Starting in one corner of the room, measure each wall in turn and write their lengths (in m) in the second column of the table. Decide how many centimetres will represent each metre on your plan, then write your scaled-down measurements (in cm) in the last column. Your completed table will look something like this:

Wall	Measured length of wall (in m)	Scaled-down length of wall (in cm)
1st	7	14
2nd	6.7	13.4
3rd	7	14
4th	6.7	13.4

Scale ⊦ 1 m ⊦

Item	Measured size (to nearest 1/10th m)	Scaled-down size (in cm)	Measured distance from the nearest wall (to nearest 1/10th m)	Scaled-down distance from this wall (in cm)
Entrance door	Width: 0.8	Width: 1.6	0.5	1
Other door	Width: 0.8	Width: 1.6	0.0	0
Teacher's table	Length: 1.5 Width: 0.8	Length: 3.0 Width: 1.6	0.5	1
Pupil's desk	Length: 1.2 Width: 0.6	Length: 2.4 Width: 1.2	Row 1 is 0.5 m from wall	1
Cupboard	Length: 0.9 Width: 0.4	Length: 1.8 Width: 0.8	0.0 (0.1 m apart)	0.0 (0.2 cm apart)
Book shelves	Length: 0.9 Width: 0.4	Length: 1.8 Width: 0.8	0.0	0.0

3 Use your scaled-down measurements to draw the walls onto your grid. If you do this carefully, your last wall will finish exactly where the first wall started! The plan on the left has been completed for the room in the table on page 14, using a scale of 1 cm = 0.5 m.

4 Decide what items in the room will go onto your plan. Don't include small things such as waste bins – but add doors, tables, desks and cupboards, for example.

Each item needs to be measured, scaled-down and recorded in a table like the one shown above. You need a new line for each item of furniture. Then draw the items in their correct places on your plan.

5 Complete your plan by using a different colour or symbol for every item. Add a **key** showing

what each one stands for, then a title and a scale line. Your finished plan will look similar to the plan below.

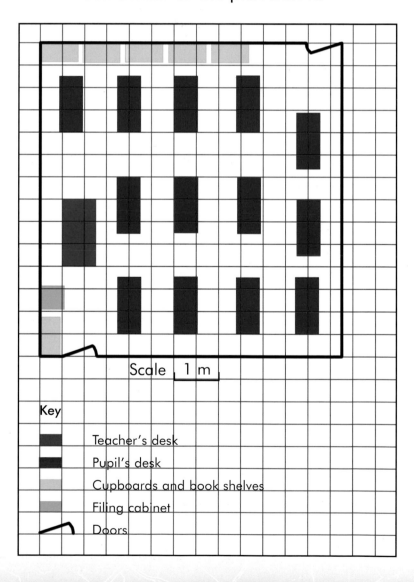

Scale | 1 | m

Key

Teacher's desk

Pupil's desk

Cupboards and book shelves

Filing cabinet

Doors

Map signs and symbols

Signs are all around us. They're a form of shorthand or coded message, giving information in a way that is easy to understand. Maps use signs as well, but we call them symbols. Map symbols help us to put a lot of information onto a map in a clear way.

Signs

Many signs give **directions** that help us to find places. The most effective signs have direction arrows and logos that can be easily understood by foreign visitors as well as local people. Examples include an elephant for a zoo, a tent for a camping site or a large letter 'H' for hospital. Probably the most important signs of all are traffic signs (see below) which help people to drive around safely.

Symbols

Landscapes have lots of different features, such as buildings, rivers, forests and fields. Maps use symbols to show as many of these features as possible. Each symbol stands for one kind of feature, and they can be drawn in four different ways (see the table below). A collection of map symbols and their meanings is called a key. The sizes of drawing, letter and line symbols never change, but shaded-area symbols can be made larger or smaller to show how big their features are.

No cycling

School crossing patrol ahead

No right turn

Zebra crossing

No entry for vehicles

Ducks crossing

▲ These traffic signs are used in the UK.

Kind of symbol	Example of symbol	Meaning of symbol
Drawing symbol	⚑	A golf course
Letter symbol	P	A post office
Line symbol	╱	A main road
Shaded-area symbol	⬭	A lake

▲ This table shows the four types of map symbols.

Do it yourself

1 Find out the meaning of these common signs.

a   b   c   d   e   f   g   h

2 The map below shows the features of a small village.
Draw a copy of this map without the words shown
in red text. Invent your own symbols for these features,
choosing them from the four symbol types shown in the
table on page 16. Add the symbols to your copy of the
map and explain what they mean by adding a key.

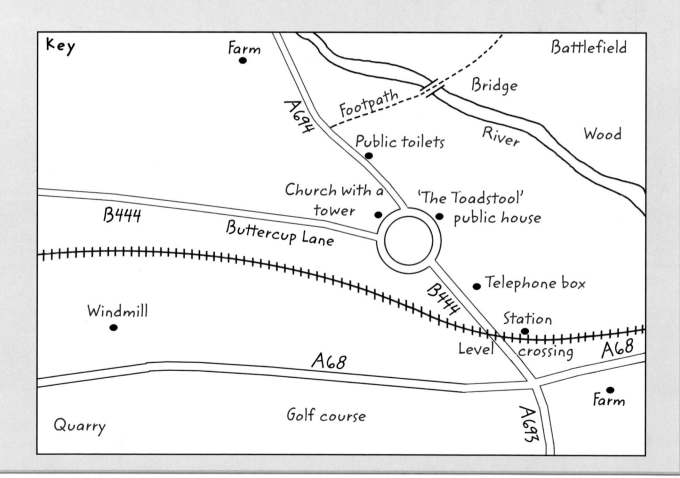

Getting your bearings

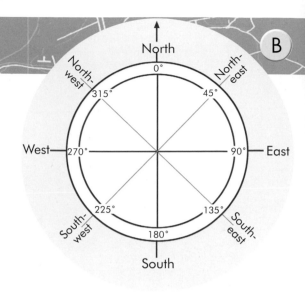

▲ *This compass rose shows different directions and bearings.*

It isn't quite as easy to get lost as it used to be! There are now lots of high-tech **navigational aids**, such as satellite navigation, to help us find our way around. But what do we do if they break down?

Sometimes we need to go back to using traditional methods, such as a map and a **magnetic compass** (see Figure A), so knowing these skills is still important.

The points of a compass

The **compass rose** in Figure B shows the four most important directions – North, South, East and West. These are **cardinal points** and their **bearings** are measured clockwise, in degrees, from North.

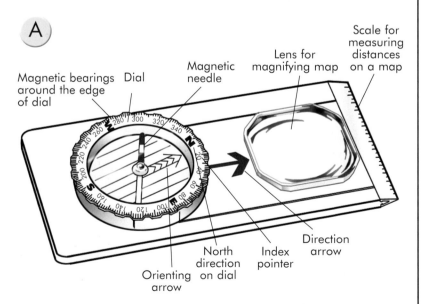

▲ *We can use a magnetic compass to work out the direction in which we are travelling. On a magnetic compass, the needle points to the North Pole.*

How to use a magnetic compass

The following steps tell you how to use a compass with a map to find the magnetic bearing of a road you want to walk down.

1 Place the compass on the map, with its edge along the road.

2 Turn the dial until N points to the direction of magnetic north on the map.

3 Take the compass off the map, turn your body until the end of the red needle points to North on the compass dial. The number of degrees shown below the red direction arrow gives the bearing of the road.

Do it yourself

1 One way to remember the cardinal points is to use a memory-aid such as "**N**aughty **E**lephants **S**quirt **W**ater!" Try to think of other **N-E-S-W** memory aids of your own.

2 Four animal statues are in a sculpture park. Use Figure C and the compass rose in Figure B to complete the compass and direction bearings table. The first line has been done for you.

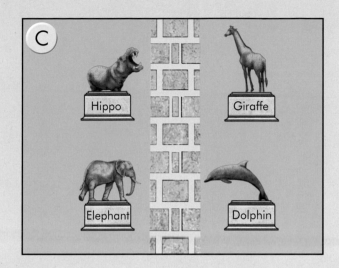

From the:	To the:	Compass direction	Compass bearing
Hippo	Elephant	South	180°
Elephant	Giraffe		
Giraffe	Dolphin		
Dolphin	Hippo		
Hippo	Giraffe		

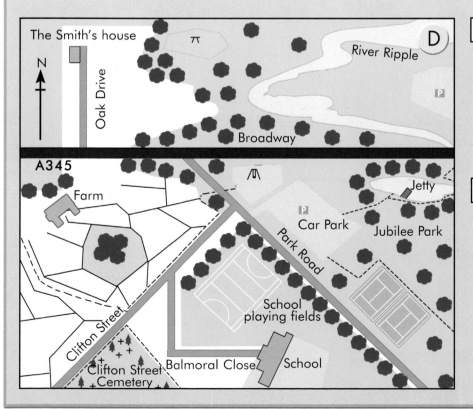

3 Figure D shows the route taken by the Smith family who live at No 6, Oak Drive, to walk to school on Balmoral Close. Which six compass directions do they follow?

4 With the help of Figure B, a map and a compass, write down the directions of your own route to school. You can use compass directions or bearings to do this.

Four-figure grid references

To find a place on a map, there has to be a way of finding locations that everyone can understand. This is why map-makers add vertical and horizontal **grid lines** to maps. Some maps label the spaces between the lines; other maps number the lines themselves.

When we use a numbered grid to find places on maps, we say that we are using 'grid references'. Finding the grid references of squares on maps like this is quite easy: always use the numbers along the bottom first, followed by the numbers up the side. It's a bit like walking along the corridor of a two-storey house before climbing up the stairs!

Figure A shows the three steps needed to give a four-figure grid reference. You would use this method to tell a friend how to find a meeting place on a map. Figure B shows you how to do the opposite – to use a grid reference to find a grid square on a map. You would use this method if you were given a grid reference to find a meeting place on a map.

A How to give the four-figure grid reference of a location on a map

1 Find the square with a bus or coach station symbol.

2 Write down the number of the line down the left side.

3 Now add the number of the line along the bottom. The four-figure grid reference is 10 33.

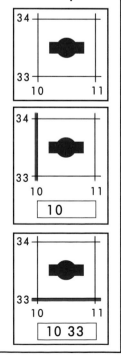

B How to use a four-figure grid reference to find a location on a map

1 To find grid square 27 48, look at the vertical line numbered 27. The square you need is to the right of this line.

2 Find the horizontal line numbered 48. The square you need is above this line.

3 The feature in grid square 27 48 is a picnic site.

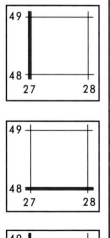

Do it yourself

1 Figure C shows a map of the area around Eaton village. Give the four-figure grid reference(s) of the map square(s) where you will find:

    a   Heaton Hall
    b   the post office
    c   Little Eaton Farm
    d   the site of a battle
    e   the bridge over a river
    f   the pub
    g   the church
    h   the school
    i   the golf course

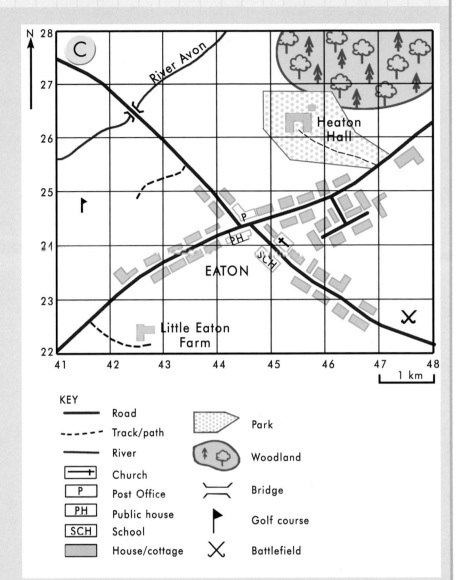

KEY

——	Road
- - - -	Track/path
——	River
Church	Church
P	Post Office
PH	Public house
SCH	School
▬	House/cottage
(dotted)	Park
Woodland	Woodland
⊐⊏	Bridge
▶	Golf course
✕	Battlefield

2 Add the following symbols to a copy of figure C:

Grid square:	Feature:	Symbol to use:
4425	windmill	⚒
4224	club house (at golf course)	CH
4223	public toilets	PC
4625	chapel	+
4427	quarry	(quarry symbol)
4226	picnic site	⋈
4127	farm (called New Farm)	⊤
4223	two new houses	▬

21

Six-figure grid references

Using four-figure grid references is a good way to find large features on a map, such as villages and woods. But we need a more accurate way to pinpoint exactly where smaller features are, such as individual buildings or telephone boxes.

The area covered by a single grid square can be quite large and is usually at least one square kilometre. Imagine if you'd arranged to meet a friend using only a four-figure reference in a large town or wooded area where you couldn't see very far. It would take you ages to find each other if you had to search the whole square kilometre before you met. Instead, we use a more accurate six-figure grid reference system to locate small places on maps.

Using six-figure grid references

Six-figure grid references work just like the four-figure system, but with two extra numbers. In a similar way to pages 20-21, Figure A shows the steps taken to give a six-figure grid reference, whilst Figure B shows how to find a location using a six-figure grid reference. You will see that the distance between the grid lines has been divided up into tenths in these diagrams. These divisions help you to pinpoint locations very accurately. But on real maps, you will have to imagine these divisions yourself!

A How to give the six-figure grid reference of a location on a map

1 Find the square with the youth hostel ▲ inside it.

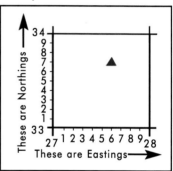

2 Write down the number of the line down the left side – then count how many tenths the youth hostel is towards the next vertical line.

3 Now add the number of the line below the youth hostel. Count how many tenths the youth hostel is towards the next horizontal line.

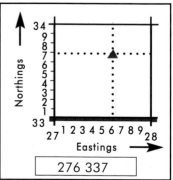

4 The six-figure grid reference is **276 337**.

B How to use a six-figure grid reference to find a location on a map

1 Find the feature located at 273 334.

2 Find the vertical line (Easting) numbered 27. The square you need is to the right of this line. Now count along 3/10 towards the next Easting. The feature is immediately north of this point.

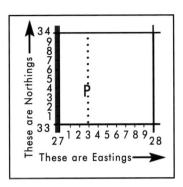

3 Find the horizontal line (Northing) numbered 33. The square you need is above this line. Now count up 4/10 towards the next Northing. The feature is immediately east of this point.

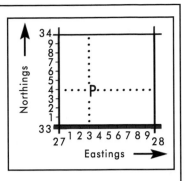

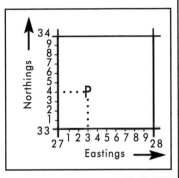

4 The feature at 273 334 is a post office (P).

Do it yourself

Figure C shows a map of the village of Burwell. Use this map to answer the following questions.

1 Which feature(s) will you find at each of the following grid-references:
 a 576 667   c 587 661
 b 596 648   d 587 677

2 Give the six-figure grid references of the following features:
 a the church nearest to the castle
 b the museum
 c the post office
 d the car park

Key
▬ Land more than 20 m high		⬨ Large house	
∿ River/stream		PH Pub	
▬ Road		P Post office	
Village		C Castle	
▭F Farm		✝ Church or chapel	
------ Path or track		Ⓧ Camp site	
⅄Mus Old windmill, now used as a museum		🅿 Parking	
		Nature reserve	

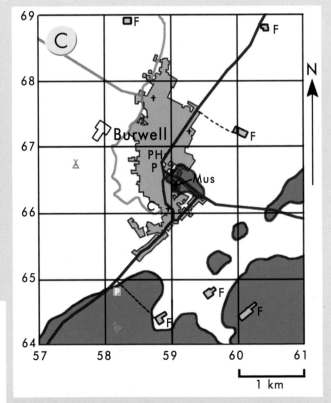

▲ A sketch map of the village of Burwell, near Cambridge.

Different kinds of maps

Maps that show landscape features, such as cities, rivers and roads, are called **topographical maps** (Figure A). But maps can also be used to show additional information, such as temperatures, rainfall distribution or population sizes.

Adding numerical information to maps can help us to see patterns and, in turn, understand the world around us. The following maps are just a few examples:

Choropleth maps

Choropleth maps use colour-shading to show information. Their colours vary from dark (showing high values) to light (showing low values). Figure B is a choropleth map showing the pattern of rainfall over the British Isles.

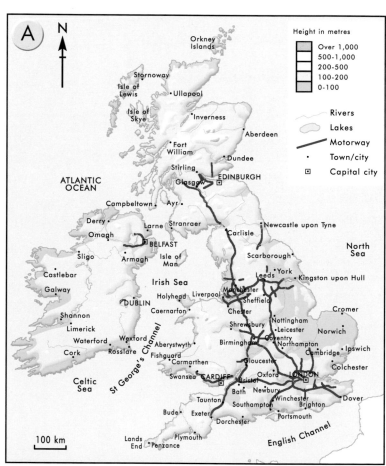

▲ This topographical map of the British Isles shows natural features such as mountains and rivers, as well as human features such as cities and motorways.

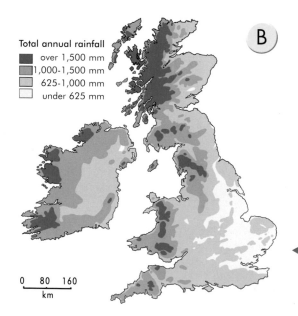

◀ On this choropleth map of the British Isles, the darkest blue shows the areas where rainfall is heaviest.

Isopleths

Other maps use lines (called **isopleths**) instead of colours to show information. These lines are used to join places that are linked in some way (see Figure C). There are many different types of isopleths including: contour lines (showing heights above sea level); isotherms (showing average temperatures); isohyets (showing average rainfall); isobars (showing air pressure); and isohels (showing hours of sunshine).

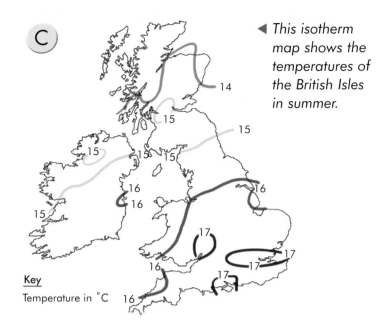

◄ This isotherm map shows the temperatures of the British Isles in summer.

Key
Temperature in °C

Flow-line maps

Lines on maps can also be used to show the movement of people or traffic. These are called **flow lines** (see Figure D). Some flow-line maps show how many people or vehicles move from one place to another by using lines of different widths.

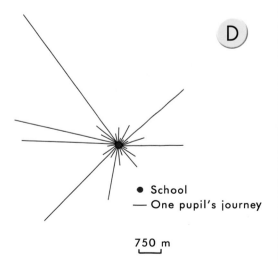

D

● School
— One pupil's journey

750 m

▲ This flow-line map shows the direction and distance that pupils in Class 5 travel to get to school.

Do it yourself

1 Figure E shows the temperatures of the British Isles in winter. Draw a copy of this map and join all the purple dots together. Then do the same for the blue, green and yellow dots. Use the same coloured crayon as the dots you are joining! The lines you have drawn are isotherms; use the key to label each one (using Figure C as an example).

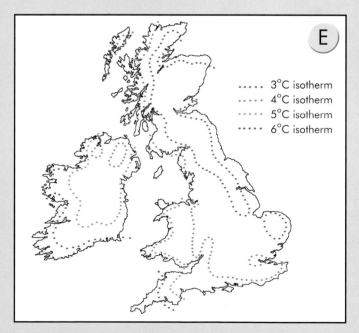

E

····· 3°C isotherm
····· 4°C isotherm
····· 5°C isotherm
····· 6°C isotherm

How to make your own map

Now you can make your own map, using the new skills you have learned. An outline map to work on is shown in Figure A. Draw a copy of this map – it can be enlarged if you wish. You may be surprised at how many map skills you now know!

1 In the spaces provided on the map:
   a draw a direction arrow showing north.
   b think of a name for your village and add a title to the map.
   c complete the scale line to show that the side of one grid square represents 500 metres in real life.

2 Number both sets of grid lines. The first Easting and Northing lines have been labelled to help you.

3 A stream starts flowing in the hills in square 2651 and joins the river at 262 487. Draw this stream, giving it a few gentle bends along its way. Label the river/stream symbol in the key.

4 The photographs in Figure B show you four important buildings in the village. Each has a grid reference telling you where it is located. Create an appropriate symbol for each building, and then draw it at its correct location on the map. Add these symbols and their meanings to the key.

5 Now invent a symbol for each of the features named in this table. Add your symbols to the map and the key.

Feature	Location
Picnic site	North-east corner of 2349
Road bridge	crossing the river in 2747
Windmill	500 m South of the picnic site
Farm	North-east corner of 2550
Track	from the farm to the A11 at 281 499
Golf course	1 km North-west of the church
Road bridge	crossing the stream in 2549 / 2649
Row of cottages	along the A10 between 270 492 and 277 487

6 Complete a copy of the table at the bottom of this page, showing the direction and distance between each pair of locations.

7 Fill a sheet of A4 paper with a 1 cm x 1 cm grid. Use the grid to practise drawing more maps using symbols and scales. Test your friends' map skills by setting them questions like the ones you have just done!

From	To	Direction	Bearing	Distance (in m)
The pub	The golf course			
The windmill	The farm			
The pub	The windmill			

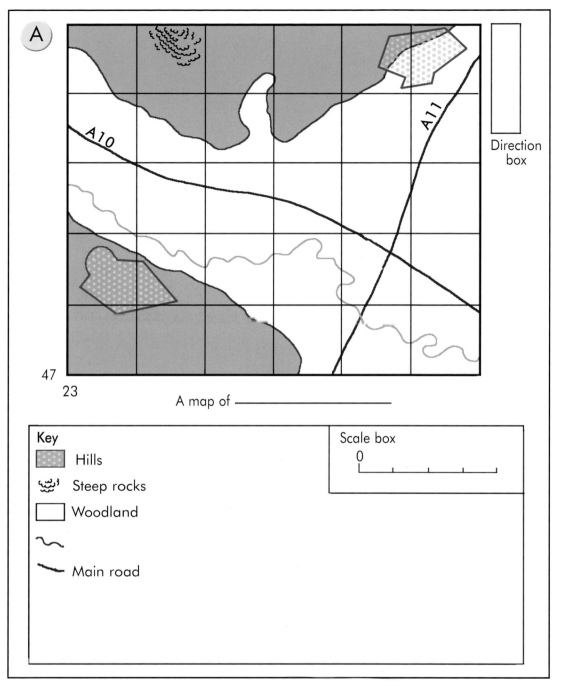

A

Direction box

A10

A11

47
23

A map of _____

Key

Hills

Steep rocks

Woodland

Main road

Scale box

0

B

The post office at
▼ 281 486

The pub at
◀ 275 487

▲ The church at
278 488

The school at
◀ 278 492

Use your skills: Island adventure

Imagine that you're a Scout or a Guide and you've come to Brownsea Island on a treasure hunt. The Scout group arrives at Pottery Pier and the Guide group arrives at Castle Pier. Look at the map below and use the directions to answer the following questions.

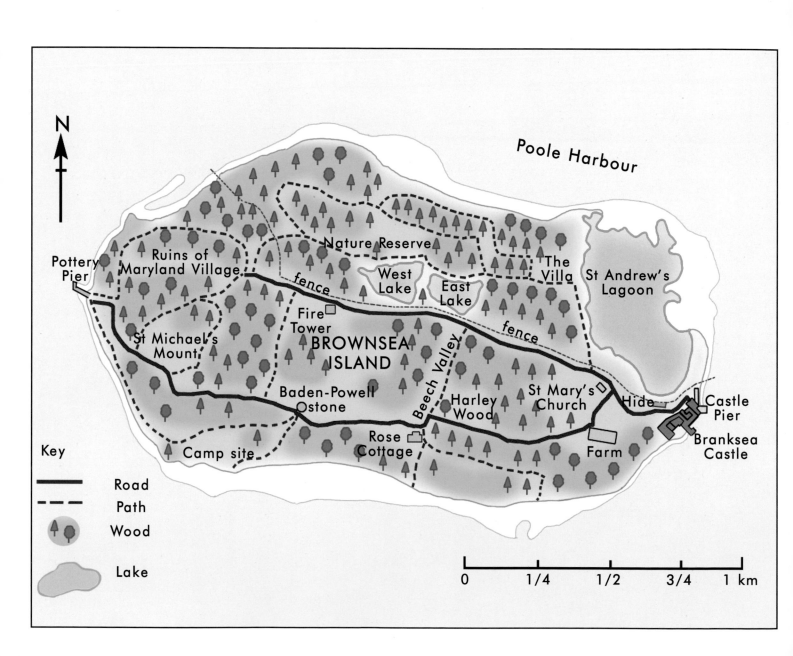

a Follow both sets of directions.

b What is the name of the building where both groups will meet?

c Which group do you think will arrive there first? Why do you think this?

The Guides' directions:

Arrive at Castle Pier, then walk along the road around Branksea Castle until you come to one of the oldest buildings on the island. Turn left at the road junction. This new road takes you past a farm before heading west. Just over 0.75 km from the junction, go round a sharp bend in the road and stop at the building on your left.

The Scouts' directions:

Arrive at Pottery Pier, and follow the path northwards around the ruins of Maryland Village. Go eastwards, along a road that passes next to the Nature Reserve fence on your left. Almost 1 km further on, turn right onto the path going south. Finally, turn right onto another road and stop at the first building you come to.

d The group that arrived second is not happy with its directions! Write them a new set of directions using paths and roads which will take them along a much shorter route.

Use your skills: Wordsearch

Make a photocopy of this page and find the key
mapwork terms hidden in the wordsearch.

22 of them are horizontal   12 of them are vertical   3 of them are diagonal

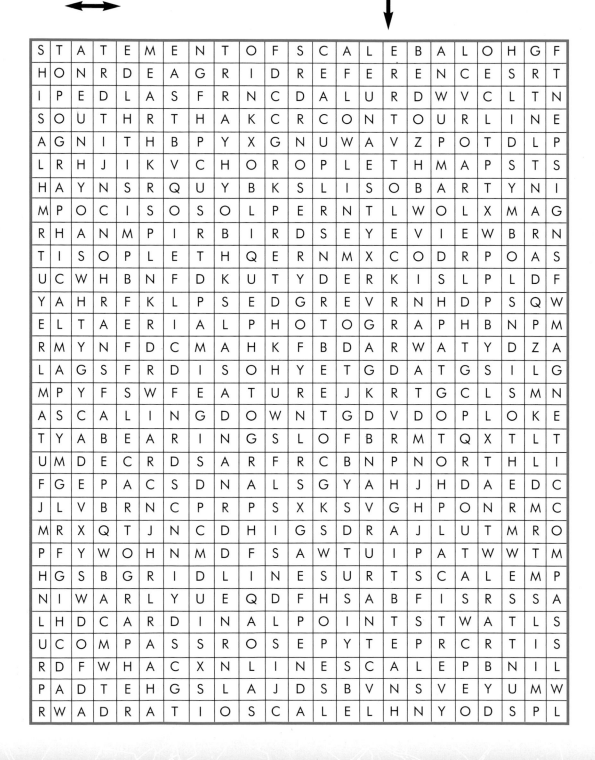

S	T	A	T	E	M	E	N	T	O	F	S	C	A	L	E	B	A	L	O	H	G	F
H	O	N	R	D	E	A	G	R	I	D	R	E	F	E	R	E	N	C	E	S	R	T
I	P	E	D	L	A	S	F	R	N	C	D	A	L	U	R	D	W	V	C	L	T	N
S	O	U	T	H	R	T	H	A	K	C	R	C	O	N	T	O	U	R	L	I	N	E
A	G	N	I	T	H	B	P	Y	X	G	N	U	W	A	V	Z	P	O	T	D	L	P
L	R	H	J	I	K	V	C	H	O	R	O	P	L	E	T	H	M	A	P	S	T	S
H	A	Y	N	S	R	Q	U	Y	B	K	S	L	I	S	O	B	A	R	T	Y	N	I
M	P	O	C	I	S	O	S	O	L	P	E	R	N	T	L	W	O	L	X	M	A	G
R	H	A	N	M	P	I	R	B	I	R	D	S	E	Y	E	V	I	E	W	B	R	N
T	I	S	O	P	L	E	T	H	Q	E	R	N	M	X	C	O	D	R	P	O	A	S
U	C	W	H	B	N	F	D	K	U	T	Y	D	E	R	K	I	S	L	P	L	D	F
Y	A	H	R	F	K	L	P	S	E	D	G	R	E	V	R	N	H	D	P	S	Q	W
E	L	T	A	E	R	I	A	L	P	H	O	T	O	G	R	A	P	H	B	N	P	M
R	M	Y	N	F	D	C	M	A	H	K	F	B	D	A	R	W	A	T	Y	D	Z	A
L	A	G	S	F	R	D	I	S	O	H	Y	E	T	G	D	A	T	G	S	I	L	G
M	P	Y	F	S	W	F	E	A	T	U	R	E	J	K	R	T	G	C	L	S	M	N
A	S	C	A	L	I	N	G	D	O	W	N	T	G	D	V	D	O	P	L	O	K	E
T	Y	A	B	E	A	R	I	N	G	S	L	O	F	B	R	M	T	Q	X	T	L	T
U	M	D	E	C	R	D	S	A	R	F	R	C	B	N	P	N	O	R	T	H	L	I
F	G	E	P	A	C	S	D	N	A	L	S	G	Y	A	H	J	H	D	A	E	D	C
J	L	V	B	R	N	C	P	R	P	S	X	K	S	V	G	H	P	O	N	R	M	C
M	R	X	Q	T	J	N	C	D	H	I	G	S	D	R	A	J	L	U	T	M	R	O
P	F	Y	W	O	H	N	M	D	F	S	A	W	T	U	I	P	A	T	W	W	T	M
H	G	S	B	G	R	I	D	L	I	N	E	S	U	R	T	S	C	A	L	E	M	P
N	I	W	A	R	L	Y	U	E	Q	D	F	H	S	A	B	F	I	S	R	S	S	A
L	H	D	C	A	R	D	I	N	A	L	P	O	I	N	T	S	T	W	A	T	L	S
U	C	O	M	P	A	S	S	R	O	S	E	P	Y	T	E	P	R	C	R	T	I	S
R	D	F	W	H	A	C	X	N	L	I	N	E	S	C	A	L	E	P	B	N	I	L
P	A	D	T	E	H	G	S	L	A	J	D	S	B	V	N	S	V	E	Y	U	M	W
R	W	A	D	R	A	T	I	O	S	C	A	L	E	L	H	N	Y	O	D	S	P	L

Glossary

Aerial photograph   A photograph taken from above the ground. Aerial photographs can be vertical (straight downwards) or oblique (downwards, but at an angle).

Bearing   A compass direction shown as a number of degrees clockwise from North.

Bird's eye view   A view of the Earth's surface as seen from just above it.

Cardinal points   The directions North, South, East and West.

Cartographer   Someone who draws maps.

Choropleth map   A map that uses colour shading to show a distribution pattern, such as the way rainfall changes across an area.

Compass rose   A diagram that shows compass directions.

Direction   The way a person or feature is pointing towards something else. Direction can be given as a compass direction or a bearing.

Feature   A part of a landscape, such as a house or a wood.

Flow line   A line that shows the direction in which people or things (such as traffic) are moving.

Grid lines   A pattern of lines on a map. One set of lines (the Northings) are vertical from top to bottom. The other set of lines (Eastings) run across the map from left to right. These lines are used to give grid references to locate places on maps.

Isopleth   A line that links places with the same value. An example is a contour joining places with the same height above sea level.

Key   A group of map symbols with an explanation of their meaning.

Landscape   All the features in a view.

Magnetic compass   A magnetic instrument showing compass directions.

Map   A scaled-down drawing that shows what a real, life-size area is like.

Navigational aids   Modern devices that help us with directions. Satellite navigation, for example, uses satellites to locate objects on Earth.

Plan   A map of a small area, such as a building or a park.

Scale   A way of showing how much smaller a map is than its real, life-size area. This can be shown in three ways: line scale, ratio scale and statement of scale.

Scaling-down   Making something small enough to put on a map.

Sign   A symbol (which can also have some words and a direction arrow) that tells people where a facility, such as a toilet or park, is located.

Symbol   A small letter or drawing showing one kind of map feature.

Topographical map   A map showing the physical and human features of an area.

Index and answers

aerial photograph 6, 7, 8, 9, 31

bearing 18, 19, 26, 31
bird's eye view 4, 5, 6, 7, 8, 9, 31

cardinal point 18, 19, 31
cartographer 6, 8, 12, 31
choropleth map 24
compass rose 18, 19, 31

direction 16, 26, 29, 31
distance 10, 22, 26

feature 4, 6, 8, 9, 12, 16, 22, 24, 26, 31
flow line 25, 31

grid line 20, 22, 26, 31
grid reference 20, 21, 22, 23

isopleth 25, 31

key 15, 16, 17, 26, 31

landscape 4, 6, 8, 12, 16, 24, 31

magnetic compass 18, 19, 31
map 4, 5, 6, 7, 8, 9, 10, 11, 12, 13, 16, 17, 18, 19, 20, 21, 22, 23, 24, 25, 26, 27, 28, 31

navigational aid 18, 31

plan 9, 14, 15, 31

scale 10, 11, 12, 13, 14, 15, 26, 31
scaling-down 12, 14, 15, 31
sign 16, 17, 31
symbol 4, 12, 16, 17, 21, 26, 31

topographical map 24, 31

Answers

p7 2) A compass direction, a key, a scale and a title. **p11 1a)** 1 km **1b)** 2 km **1c)** 9 km **1d)** approx 6 km **1e)** 8 km **1f)** 6 km **1g)** 48 km² **p 17 1a)** Hospital with an Accident and Emergency Unit **1b)** Wheelchair access available **1c)** Escalator (going up) **1d)** Male and female toilets **1e)** Use washing cycle with water no hotter than 40°C **1f)** No dogs allowed **1g)** Danger! Inflammable material! **1h)** Information centre **p19 2)** North-east, 45°; South, 180°; North-west, 315°; East, 90° **3)** South, East, South-east, South-west, South, East. **p21 1a)** 4526 **1b)** 4424 **1c)** 4222 **1d)** 4722 **1e)** 4226 **1f)** 4424 **1g)** 4523 and 4524 **1h)** 4423 and 4523 **1i)** 4124 **p23 1a)** camp site **1b)** farm **1c)** castle **1d)** church or chapel **2a)** 589 661 **2b)** 591 664 **2c)** 588 667 **2d)** 582 648 **p26 6)** From the pub to the golf course – North-west, approx 315°, approx 900 m. From the windmill to the farm – North-east, 45°, 1,500 m. From the pub to the windmill – West, 270°, 1,800 m. **p29 b)** Rose Cottage **c)** The Guides, because they have less far to go. **p30 Horizontal** (22 entries, in order from top to bottom) Statement of scale, Grid references, South, Contour line, Choropleth maps, Isobar, Isosol, Birds eye view, Isopleth, Aerial photograph, Isohyet, Feature, Scaling down, Bearings, North, Landscape [printed backwards], Grid lines, Scale, Cardinal points, Compass rose, Line scale, Ratio scale, **Vertical** (12 entries, in order from left to right) Topographical maps, Cartographer, East, Map [printed backwards], Oblique photograph, Flow line, Vertical photograph [printed backwards], Symbols, Isotherm, West, Signs, Magnetic compass, **Diagonal** (3 entries, in order from top left to bottom right) Grid, Plan, Compass [printed backwards].